NUMEROLOGY

Numbers have valid meanings. Properly interpreted, they can provide a route for life's journey. This book reveals how to analyse your name and birthdate numerically for exploring character and assessing future prospects.

NUMEROLOGY
The Secret Power of Numbers

by

MARY ANDERSON

SAMUEL WEISER INC.
740 Broadway, New York, N.Y. 10003

First published 1972
Third Impression 1977
Second Edition, revised, enlarged
and reset, 1979

ISBN 0 85030 183 1 (UK)
ISBN 0 87728 442 3 (USA)

Photoset by
Specialised Offset Services Ltd., Liverpool
Printed and bound in Great Britain by
Weatherby Woolnough, Wellingborough,
Northamptonshire

CONTENTS

FOREWORD

We all use numbers every day, but few of us think that there is more to numbers than their general use as a medium of measurement. In fact, numbers have their own inner characteristics and meanings and understanding these leads us down a path of discovery, even self-discovery, which can pay us handsome dividends in terms of happiness and success.

To those of an enquiring mind who want to know why, I would just say 'try for yourself'; I shall be giving you all the tools you need for the work. You can then do some venturesome exploring and who can say how absorbed you may become in your journey of discovery to the secret inner worlds?

These are the same worlds of abstract design in which mathematicians of old, like Pythagoras, laboured to bring the world a workable system based on the numbers one to nine. Later researchers have added two master numbers, eleven and twenty-two.

It is interesting to note that Pythagoras said 'Nature geometrizes', and the great psychologist Jung stressed that numbers, instead of being the product of invention, were found or discovered. He said, in fact, that they were spontaneous productions of the unconscious and that the latter uses number as an ordering factor.

The origin of both the alphabet and numbers seems lost in the mists of antiquity, but so far as we are concerned, numbers have valid meanings and so can guide us in assessing both people and situations.

We are all interested in ourselves. Numbers provide us with interesting tools for exploring ourselves and our own potential and destiny.

This is not all. We can obtain valuable guidelines as to our future, our career, happiness, health, success. Numbers, their analysis and understanding, put into our hands a route map to guide us on our journey through life as well as a basic 'map' showing our particular situation at birth.

Given this data, there is no longer any need to hesitate or waver, lose our way and waste our time, we have only to follow our number guidelines.

Words are symbols of thoughts, and like numbers they communicate ideas. Words can be transformed into numbers for each letter has a numerical value of its own just as each number has a letter value.

So let us get to work now and give you the basic meanings of the numbers.

CHAPTER ONE

THE MEANING OF NUMBERS

Number One

The person who has number 1 on any of the main positions of birthday, expression, destiny or reality, and so predominant in his numberscope, is a dynamic personality, independent, original, creative, a hard worker. He gets things done, encourages, advises and drives others. If he will use these qualities positively, his life will be successful.

This number is ruled by the Sun, and stands for all things masculine, such as courage, leadership, decision and willpower. Number 1 people are predominantly mental types and are introverted. Those who have number 1 strong can only fail if they are indecisive, lacking in confidence, lazy and allow themselves to be led by others. They can also fail if they become over-positive, dominant, egotistic and intolerant.

When applied to future events, number 1 indicates new starts, the launching of new projects, personal or business. Success if the past is left behind, a time to be determined, active and courageous.

Affinities — 2, 4, 7. Colours — yellow/gold/bronze. Fortunate days — Sunday and Monday.

Number Two

Numbers 1 and 2 go together, they are polarities for number 2 is as essentially female as number 1 is masculine. Number 2 people, that is people with 2 predominant in their numberscope, should ideally exhibit the best of the womanly qualities, that is gentleness, tact, adaptability, understanding and wisdom.

Number 2 is ruled by the Moon, and so to you the home, family and peace and harmony in relationships are very important. They should be the ones to make for harmony and beauty in their surroundings, they should never push for things, but gain them through their quiet, gentle, diplomatic ways and capacity to handle others.

Number 2 people can fail if they fall into negative ways, accepting everything which is dealt out to them without protest, being over-tolerant, obsessive about detail and worrisome, not being able to adapt themselves to others and losing out by being moody, touchy and easily upset.

People with this vibration predominant can be either too 'bottled up' or over-emotional, they need to keep a balance for success and happiness. Their warmth, sympathy and understanding attract others.

Regarding future events, number 2 warns of the need for caution, a wait-and-see attitude, the time for decision is not yet.

Affinities – 1 and 7. Colours – all pale and

pastel shades. Fortunate days – Sunday and Monday.

Number Three

Number 3 always relates to self-expression, and if number 3 is predominant in your numberscope you must always try for personal self-expression in creative ways, for this number gives you talent where writing and speaking are concerned.

Number 3 endows its children with a basically happy, optimistic, carefree nature, they must not be imprisoned or forced into too practical ways for this number tells that they were born to encourage and entertain others.

A creative outlet is essential for success through acting, singing, dancing, music or other forms of creativity.

The number 3 is essentially related to Jupiter, planet of abundance, joy, good luck, so you feel the need for breadth of contacts, social life, friends and a job which is not too practical and down to earth.

Failure comes to the number 3 if you do not develop your potential, if instead of being a joy-bringer you are a pessimist and a killjoy. You can also fail by being too restless, by never sticking to anything, and by worrying unduly you can make yourself and others into nervous wrecks.

Overdevelopment of your basic characteristics can also lead to failure through a tendency to self-advertisement, boasting and conceit. Snobbism and cynicism are also negative 3 traits.

Success comes to the number 3 when you develop and use your gifts, then your life brings happiness to others and you are fulfilled yourself. For the future it gives the green light and suggests Lady Luck is around.

Affinities – 6 and 9. Colours – all shades of violet and purple. Fortunate day – Thursday.

Number Four

If you have someone in your family who is predominantly a 3 person, and another member who is very much a 4 person, you will continually be reminded of their differences, for these two numbers are almost mutually exclusive, although each could give much to the other.

Number 4 people are predominantly strong-willed and serious, for 4 is the number of the will and so 4 people can be powerfully constructive, true builders, willing to work and attend to details, or they can be equally powerfully destructive.

Naturally number 4 people will be successful if they are prepared to work to develop their skills in order to be of service to others. They should be reliable, responsible and patient, for upon their work and sound constructive abilities many vast edifices are based. Routine, detail and system are very important to them and they dislike change unless advised of it well in advance. Tenacious, obstinate and determined, they get things done.

Number 4 is related to the planet Uranus in its more Saturnine construction, and therefore number 4 is rated a relatively restrictive number and vibrates on an earth quality.

It may be said that the strongly 4 person has to face definite limitations and restrictions, but his powerful willpower and determination, allied with creative imagination, enable him to override difficulties and reach success – a service of some kind is often the best bet for him.

He can fail if he uses his willpower in purely destructive ways to rebel against practically everything, to argue and debate endlessly and even use violence to reach his ends.

On the negative side, too, he can be stubborn to a fault, unreliable, weak, careless and lacking in concentration. For the future it shows the time to slow down and work for change in the future.

Affinities – 2 and 8. Colour – grey. Fortunate days – Saturday/Sunday, Monday.

Number Five

Number 5 predominant in the numberscope gives quickness of thought and action, a love of freedom, change and variety. These people are truly mercurial, they are progressive in thought and hate to be tied down to routine or monotony.

They flourish where things are going on and generally choose a public career related to travel, salesmanship, the creative arts, adventure, communication in one of its forms.

Number 5 is ruled by the planet Mercury, and so the number 5 person has a brighter than average mind and has to use his creative powers constructively to be happy and successful. Thought and communication are very important to him and he can, therefore, fall down on this vibration by using his mind destructively and so make himself ill and others unhappy.

Negatively he can be destructive and pessimistic or else just plain unreliable, deceitful, a confidence trickster, using his glib tongue and power over speech to fool and defraud others. When acting negatively he avoids all responsibility and tries never to 'carry the can'.

Number 5 is also the number of sex attraction and magnetism, and number 5 people are generally strongly attracted to the opposite sex.

For the future it demands 'get about', move, change, communicate, invest in your own talents, take a chance.

Affinities – all groups, but especially their own '5'. Colours – all light, shining colours. Fortunate day – Wednesday.

Number Six

Number 6 is the number of the romantic idealist. Number 6 is sympathetic, attractive and loving. It inclines the person who has this number predominant in their numberscope to strive for love, their own home and hearth fire.

You'll have a very strong desire for harmony and beauty around you, whether this is in your home, community or group. You are basically conservative in your views and ideas.

Your ideals always drive you on to seek for improvement in everything you touch, and you have a flair for beauty, colour and art.

With this number strong you are essentially a practical person and can accept responsibility, whether in the home or in the wider sphere of community or organization.

Happiness to the number 6 is essentially sharing and harmony in relationships, hence the importance of forming the right relationships. It is a number ruled by the planet Venus so that there is artistic ability as well, which is often expressed in the home environment and in clothes if not actually in other creative work.

Success comes through diplomatic balancing and handling of the difficult temperaments the number 6 will inevitably encounter in their immediate surroundings, and the giving of willing service.

Failure arises through an insistence on your own ideals, a too narrow, exclusive

attitude to loved ones, friends and
possessions. There can be jealousy and
interference with others and continual
complaints which lead to quarrels.

For the future this number shows that
matters have to be adjusted in the home and
possibly between partners, as it is a number
which rules both marriage and divorce. 'Do
not delay' is the message.

Affinities – 6, 3 and 9. Colours – blue and
pink. Fortunate day – Friday.

Number Seven

While number 6 people are essentially
extrovert, needing companionship, number 7
people are introverted and the thinkers,
mystics and philosophers of this world.
Understandably then, you who come under
its vibration tend to be silent, secretive,
selective, solitary and aloof. You are strongly
individualistic, sense a great deal, but say
little.

Number 7 is ruled by Neptune, the
inspirational, illusive planet, the planet of the
heights and depths. Those with 7 strong can
be markedly creative and artistic if they use
their gifts positively.

You have the capacity to see through
things, to reach a more spiritual reality, you
do not fit in easily with the hustle and bustle
of the modern world.

Essential to the success of the number 7
are peace and quiet and communion with
their inner selves. Sacrifice of some kind

usually enters into their lives whether as children or adults, for this is the number of soul growth.

When we spoke of the heights and the depths, the heights alluded to the inspirational/spiritual insight conferred by the number. The depths referred to the illusionary side of the 7, and the wearing of rose-coloured spectacles.

The illusionary side leads to the desire to escape from reality and this can come about in various ways through refusal to face the self and problems as they really are. This can lead to drugs, drink, promiscuity, illness.

Living up to the highest in your nature you can be the mystic or creative artist and find success through following the truths which you unearth from your inner self.

When this number comes up for the future, a beautiful aura of self-deception can make life difficult. Relationships do not last, contracts should not be entered into. There is a need for self-examination and facing the truth.

Affinities – 1, 2 and 4. Colours – pastel shades, white and pale grey. Fortunate days – Sunday and Monday.

Number Eight

People who come strongly under this number are realists, good organizers, energetic, ambitious and capable. Their vibration is of earthly and material power, so you number 8 people are often attracted to 'big business' and to the organizations which stand for this.

You are people who have a good eye for value, you are discriminating and authoritative, prepared to work relentlessly towards your goal.

If working for material power only you will not find success, you have to incorporate ideals and doing things for others into your philosophy then you are better prepared to withstand the obstacles and disappointments you will have to surmount to achieve your ambitions.

Mistakes can be made on this vibration if number 8 tries to drive too hard, yourself and others, and misses out on the spiritual side of life. You find success if you will temper justice with mercy and do not neglect the emotional and spiritual.

Number 8 is often associated with marriage, for number 8s are more dependent upon others than they would like to admit. You need love and affection, but find it difficult to express your feelings.

Marriage in this connection has often something to do with security and money. Number 8 is ruled by the planet Saturn, so number 8s have to work and keep working to achieve their goal and stay there.

Success for them is to be found in the world of material values and power.

In predicting for the future, number 8 warns that this is no time to stand still. One must go ahead but be prepared to work and take responsibility. Marriage is a serious affair based on financial security.

Affinities – 2, 4, 11, 22. Colours – all dark shades from brown to black. Fortunate day – Saturday.

Number Nine

With number 9 we complete the circle of the numbers from 1 to 9. People who have number 9 predominant have energy and drive, optimism and generosity coupled with great compassion. It is the vibration of energy which is to be used for universal service and love.

You are never pretty or small, but grasp broad principles and contacts. You are strongly intuitional and creative, but your true fulfilment only comes through service, tolerance and a capacity to be fair in all your dealings. You are leaders and have the drive, courage and optimism to pull success out of disaster.

You succeed through using your energy and drive in fields which will give you broad scope for usefulness, and in particular those under this number are often drawn to travel communications and foreign fields of service and enterprise; some field where your drive, imagination and sense of adventure will not be stifled and where your need to serve will bring you happiness and fulfilment.

You can fail if you allow selfishness and narrowmindedness to enter into your thinking and attitudes. You will find life tries you on these scores.

Number 9 is associated with the planet Mars, and so gives a strong character, independence and assurance.

When this number is shown for the future, nothing new should be begun, for 9 being the end of a cycle shows this is the time to pick up loose ends and gird the loins for new ventures in the future. It represents termination where a relationship is concerned.

Affinities – 3 and 6. Colours – rose through to red. Fortunate day – Tuesday.

Number Eleven

This is considered a master vibration and you who have this number strong have spiritual insight, are idealistic and visionary and, being ahead of your time, are not easily accepted or understood by others.

You are 'tuned in' to higher forces. Your minds are inventive, progressive, intuitive. You are searchers and seekers after truth, so unconventional and unorthodox in your beliefs. You are always a law unto yourselves and have to go your own way in life.

Success comes to you in life when you uncover truths about yourself, others and life, which can benefit the race and humanity as a whole. You are often lonely for there are few at present who follow this inner path with dedication. This number is associated with the planet Uranus.

Failure can come on this vibration fairly easily for it is a master vibration and proves too strong for many, turning them into cranks and crackpots, easily taken in by any charlatan or offer of a new heaven on earth.

Number 11 should remember their high opportunities and stress the use of their intuition and teaching others the values they have proven.

When 11 appears for the future, it is a time both to teach and to learn, to express ideas, however progressive and radical.

Affinities – 2, 4, 8 and 22. Colours – all electric shades. Fortunate days – Sunday and Monday.

Number Twenty-two

This is another master vibration. As number 11 is a higher octave of number 2, the Moon, so number 22 is a higher octave of number 4.

You people who have number 22 strong in your numberscopes are idealists and have tremendous potential for realizing your ideals. You are idealists *de luxe*, but also have the capacity to put your ideals into practice for you can see the scheme as a whole.

Failure and difficulty arise on this number if you allow yourself to be bogged down by details and by lesser minds with narrower vision.

Often, too, you fear to tear down what you or others have erected for fear of failure, but you should have courage, for emphasis with this number is on building, creating, making master plans and using vision.

As a future indicator it implies 'Yes, go

ahead, but do not allow others to deter you, you may have to destroy before you can build; do not be afraid, for you will succeed.'

Affinities – 2, 11 and 8. Colours – yellow/gold, and electric blue. Fortunate day – Monday.

CHAPTER TWO

WORDS AND NUMBERS

Now we have to show how numbers are related to language, and this is done by setting out the primary digits 1 to 9 and simply placing the letters of the alphabet under them.

```
1 2 3 4 5 6 7 8 9
A B C D E F G H I
J K L M N O P Q R
S T U V W X Y Z
```

Name Analysis
In analysing a name, three major operations are necessary to obtain three different numbers, all of which have their separate meanings as related to *you*.

1. *Your AMBITION or Inner Urge Number* is called the ideality by some numerologists. This is found by the addition of the vowels in your name. Vowels are A E I O U, and if there is no vowel in the name, Y becomes a vowel.

2. *Your PERSONALITY number.* This represents the outer you, sometimes called the impression or appearance number. (The 'impression' you make.) This is found by the

addition of the consonants in your name.

3.   *Your EXPRESSION number.* These are the abilities with which you were endowed at birth.

Always use the name you were given at birth, even if adopted. This is your true vibration, other names taken add vibrations, but life runs on your original name and no other, this is *you*; your parents, believe it or not, were inspired to give you the right name.

We can now set up a name and analyse it into its components. First of all numbers must be reduced to a single digit.

$$= 6 \qquad = 6 \qquad = 6+6 = 12 = 1+2 = 3$$
$$\underline{} \qquad \underline{} 3 = \textit{Ambition or}$$

Vowels   5+1   1 + 5   *Drive Number*

J E A N H A R V E Y

Consonants 1 + 5   8 + 9+4 + 7
$$= 6 \qquad = 28 = 2+8 = 10 = 1.$$

Consonants totalled = 6+1 = 7
7 = *Impression Number*

Totalling the vowels and consonants together once they are reduced to a single digit gives an *Expression Number* of 1, i.e. 3 Ambition + 7 Impression = 10 = 1. Summarizing, then – Jean Harvey has:

3, drive or ambition, the inner urge.

7, impression or appearance number.

1, expression or attitude plus abilities.

So this tells us that at heart, Jean is a sociable, fun-loving, talented type. She loves people around her, a home, family, children and friends; she can paint, write or express herself in some other creative way (her 3 ambition).

However, the immediate impression she gives others is of someone rather aloof, chilly and reserved (7 impression). She is the type who will wait and see how she likes you at the first meeting. If she finds she has anything in common she will unbend and be interesting if she is sure of her ground.

With a 1 expression she throws herself into achieving what she wants out of life and concentrates on doing well whatever she undertakes.

In her own sphere she will be a leader inclined to want to do things her own way in an original, independent manner. However, her desire to be liked (3 ambition) and her sensitivity will serve as welcome brakes on any tendency on her part to be too bossy or selfish, at least in too obvious a manner.

However, it is wise to remember that *any* number can be used negatively, and so a person may show forth the unpleasant side of a number rather than its constructive vibration.

$$
\begin{array}{ll}
10 = 1 \qquad 14 = 5 & \text{Vowel total} = 1+9 = 10 = 1 \\
& \qquad\qquad\qquad 5+9 = 14 = 5 \end{array} = 6
$$

$$
\begin{array}{ll}
\dfrac{}{1 + 9} \quad \dfrac{}{5 + 9} \\
\text{D A V I D} \quad \text{W E I R} \\
\dfrac{4 + 4 + 4}{12 = 3} \quad \dfrac{5 + 9}{14 = 5}
\end{array}
$$

6 = *Ambition Number*

Consonant
   total   =

$$
\begin{array}{l}
4+4+4 = 12 = 3 \\
5 + 9 = 14 = 5 \end{array} = 8
$$

8 = *Impression Number*

So David Weir has a 6 ambition number and an 8 impression number derived from the consonant total. The two added together give $6 + 8 = 14 = 5$ *Expression*.

From this we gather that David Weir is home-loving, conscientious and diplomatic, he will want to help others and at the same time will want encouragement, love, home and family, and adequate remuneration for any work he undertakes. (The ambition number 6.)

His outward personality is powerful and inspires confidence in others, he likes good clothes and the company of those who count.

Combining the two vibrations as 'the tools he has brought to use' we have a 5 total, and this implies that he has quickness and agility both mentally and physically. He will not want to be too tied down, the 5 likes change and variety. His ambition number will incline him to work for others and in partnership, perhaps as a doctor or other therapist, where his versatility and attractive, confident approach would be helpful.

It has to be remembered that the inner urge will count a great deal, this is what the person really wants to do, his drive is the secret hidden mainspring of all his actions.

Whereas a number 6 ambition will want love, a home and family, will want to help others and bear responsibility, the number 5 ambition will desire to be free and progressive, to use his creative gifts.

Number 5 will not make the ordinary husband or father; although he is fond of the young and romance, marriage for him will have to include intellectual interests in common, in the same way as the number 6 ambition will desire artistic and cultural interests in common.

The total of the consonants and the vowels shows what the person does best and his general mental approach.

For instance, a person with a 1 expression would never do well working in a subordinate position, in an ordinary humdrum job without any chance of using his creative and original ideas, his capacity for concentration and hard work. He travels best alone.

The frequency with which numbers appear in a name or the lack of them is of great importance, for remember, every letter has a number, every number has a specific characteristic.

When tabulated these show what the person has or lacks in his makeup. These are unconscious factors, and if you have a belief in karma and reincarnation these, where lacking, indicate weaknesses to be made good during this life and where present benefits are piled up from the past.

It seems only too true that life tests us on our weaknesses!

Taking DAVID WEIR as an example we can set up his specialized traits as:

D A V I D W E I R
4 1 4 9 4 5 5 9 9

1	x	1
0	x	2
0	x	3
3	x	4
2	x	5
0	x	6
0	x	7
0	x	8
3	x	9

Here we see that David Weir has a predominance of 4s and 9s, the 4 representing the practical skilled worker or technologist and the 9 representing the humanitarian and service in a wide universal sense. Both these are numbers of service and the 4 has a particular slant regarding health.

David has quite a few numbers lacking, but these may be made up on the major positions, in fact the 5 is also the number of his expression, likewise 6 is his heart number.

However, 2, 3 and 7 are not made up so we can conclude that David Weir will find the situations symbolized by these numbers cropping up in his life and to a lesser extent those other missing numbers will also make their lack felt, for these are his stumbling blocks.

His natural talents are:

4 A person who is good at routine, detail and system, he is a practical builder and worker, his concentration and judgment are good.

9 He has compassion and sensitivity, he is kind, sympathetic and generous, he has literary or artistic ability and enjoys travel and broad contacts.

Numbers lacking:

2 He tends to lack the idea of co-operation and does not always consider others as much as he should.

3 He tends to be impatient, scatters his forces and may suffer from an inferiority complex.

6 The question of responsibility, particularly in the home, will come up in his life at some time, and there may be trouble in this respect.

7 He is not an analytic type, the caution and tendency to look under the surface for hidden meanings is absent. He may well be happier for this.

8 In his case this is largely made up by the 4s, which give him the application and practical ability also endowed by the number 8. He will not be too intense nor will he drive too much and worry about money.

The numbers always have the same meaning, it is just that their interpretation varies according to where they are found in the name.

A brief outline is given of the intensification table, or what the presence or lack of a number means in the name, to help you work your own traits out. You can add to these from the explanations given earlier as to the meaning of numbers.

Talents

Many of these numbers give:

1 Leadership, pioneering, originality, independence, drive.

2 Diplomacy, co-operation, sensitivity, moodiness, indecision, consideration.

3 Sociability, self-expression, optimism, imagination, the spoken or written work, so ability along these lines.

4 Practicality, application, work, economy, restriction, health, tendency to be stubborn.

5 Freedom, variety, adaptability, change, attraction to the opposite sex, resourcefulness, highly strung.

6 Love, ideals, domesticity, service, protection, marriage, adjustment, balance, artistic ability.

7 Powers of analysis, introspection, secretiveness, faith, wisdom, peace, quiet.

8 Executive ability, good judgment, material power, success, ambition.

9 Universal love, sense of brotherhood and service, compassion, understanding, artistic literary ability.

Faults

Few of these numbers give:

1 Lack of ambition, independence, originality and ambition. Too much thought for self, lazy.

2 Lack of co-operation or consideration for others, little sense of harmony, rhythm. Tact and diplomacy missing.

3 Lack of patience, difficulty in expressing the self. Lack of imagination and a quick temper, tries to do too much. Perhaps an inferiority complex.

4 Dislike of work, detail application, concentration, a tendency to impatience.

5 Dislikes change or fears it, little curiosity, hangs on to old situations and things.

6 Lack of ideals, a neglect of duty, unwillingness to assume responsibility.

7 Does not analyse, is not introspective, ignores intuitions.

8 Lacks good judgment and a sound money sense, can worry about money unduly or be completely carefree.

9 Has a narrow outlook, lack of compassion, understanding, little interest in others or the good of humanity.

CHAPTER THREE

YOUR DESTINY PATTERN

Up to now we have analysed a name into its component parts and shown the traits and characteristics as indicated by the numbers.

Now we have to go a little further and interpret your birthdate also, for this indicates the job you were sent to do, your purpose in life, and the path you must walk to fulfil this mission.

The path of destiny is found by adding the day, month and year of birth and reducing to a single digit, unless this is one of the master numbers 11 and 22, which are not reduced.

We will take someone born on 6 October 1947.

Day 6   Month 10   Year 1947
  = 6   = 1   = 3   = 10   = 1

This person's destiny or birth path is 1. 1 is the number of the pioneer, the individualist, he will always find himself in situations where he has to stand alone, make his own decisions, he should not allow others to butt in on his decisions.

Now let us consider the birthday 4 March 1930.

Day 4   Month 3   Year 1930
  = 4   = 3   = 4   = 11

This is a master vibration or overtone, and

where it comes as a destiny influence it can be reduced to the simple 2 unless the person wishes to face up to the potential of the 11. Here the stress is on intuition, teaching and idealism. People born under this number are interested in the unusual, they are searchers and seekers after the truth, they may have radical views, but they have to live up to their ideals and so they may be lonely, or living negatively, eccentric.

YOUR PATH OF DESTINY IS YOUR CHALLENGE – LOOK BELOW AND FIND YOURS

A 1 Path of Destiny – The Pioneer

This is the number of the pioneer, so your path must be original and give you independence, you must be at the helm and make your own decisions.

You have keen perception, good concentration and ability to get ahead and overcome any obstacle to your success when you use your own creative ideas.

This is one of the birth path numbers which gives every prospect of success and an interesting vital life.

However, avoid living negatively, either by being lazy and indecisive or else by being too dominant and selfish.

A 2 Path of Destiny – Co-operation

Your life will lead you into situations where

tact and diplomacy are necessary. You
cannot live without others, and should
realize that helping others and co-operating
with them will bring you the things that you
need.

Your innate understanding and
consideration for others will pay off every
time. Be patient and friendly, provide the
necessary 'oil' to the machinery of life.

Collect information and be prepared to
work at detail in order to be of service to
others. Stick to the tried ways and be
cautious in making changes. Your success is
tied up with the success of others, either
those in the home or in the group or
community.

Avoid living negatively through being too
emotional or moody, gossiping or betraying
confidences.

A 3 Path of Destiny – Individual Self-
Expression
Life will put in your way opportunities for
self-expression, and you should take them,
even if this is only an optimistic encouraging
word to your friends, family and neighbours.

Write, speak, or use your potential in any
creative way, for you were meant to be a
bringer of joy to the world. Cultivate your
associations and help others to be of good
cheer.

Life for you should be expansive and
successful if you have developed your creative
powers, then you will have achieved the

luxury and beautiful surroundings which your soul craves.

Avoid the negative traits of being dominant and boastful, pessimistic, critical or cynical.

A 4 Path of Destiny – Practical Organization

Your path is likely to entail you in a great deal of 'hard grind'. Even if your other numbers show you have riches, their possession will entail your doing a lot of hard work and giving much attention to detail. Moreover, there are bound to be times in your life when you are very much restricted by the need for economy, duty and responsibility, even perhaps by your health.

However, do not turn your head away in disgust for your contribution to the general weal is absolutely essential, for this is a cornerstone number and you are likely to be well rewarded for the amount of hard work, sheer grit and endurance you have had to put in. Things come slowly to you.

Be responsible, efficient and prepared to work hard, and you will be a success. Don't fall down on duties and obligations, you are the builder for the future.

A 5 Path of Destiny – Experience and Change

You will never find yourself in a rut for yours is the path of freedom, change, variety, travel and adaptation to life's vicissitudes. You are given this number to learn the right way of using freedom.

If you think of anything as too permanent, you will soon find that this is not so; although you should not make changes for the sake of change, always thinking that the grass on the other side of the fence is greener.

Learn foreign languages, be alert to what is going on, keep up with the world, seek new ventures and untried paths, tackle things with ingenuity. Use your capacity to get things going and keep them moving forward progressively. You are one of the progressives of the numberscope, be free, but don't neglect your roots.

You will have fulfilled your pattern if you have been prepared for change and a full life, if you have packed it full of experience.

Avoid giving in to every self-indulgent whim, be prepared to be responsible and not too casual about money – even you have to earn it.

A 6 Path of Destiny – Responsibility/Service
At least some of the cares of the world are bound to be yours for you were born to be the comforter, the diplomat, the adjuster of inharmonious circumstances. You have to learn to serve lovingly, cheerfully, efficiently, maybe within the home where everyone's comfort and happiness depends upon your tact and wisdom, or in a wider circle or community.

Without your capacity for loving and

sympathy the world would be a poor place indeed.

No matter how independent you are, your destiny will always push you to assuming responsibility and the care of others, whether this is solely in marriage or in the professional or commercial world.

Your success comes from the love which others show you, as well as the financial rewards which will be yours.

You can fail if you refuse to accept responsibility, if you try to dominate or possess others, forcing them to your way of thinking, making them emotionally dependent on you.

A 7 Path of Destiny – Mental Analysis – Wisdom

Yours is the path of the thinker and philosopher. You will find yourself naturally drawn to studying meanings and theories, for your task is to ferret out the truth behind the appearance and in so doing to attain wisdom.

Not for you the rush and the dash of modern life, you function best behind the scenes and as a lone operator. Somehow you have to learn to be alone and like it at times, for it is essential to your inner growth. Only in the silence will you find the answers to life's problems. In understanding that all answers have to come from within will you be able to guide others.

The secret, the antique and the mysterious

will always have their charm for you, and
you will be successful in so far as you learn to
operate from your inner centre. Never rush
into anything; accept your partnerships in a
philosophical manner.

You can make things difficult for yourself
if you fear failure and loneliness, if you are
unreasonable, moody and unwilling to learn
the secrets of life in whatever field you
investigate them.

Your success comes through specialization
and the development of your innate skill and
wisdom.

An 8 Path of Destiny – Money –
Commercial Power

If you have an 8 destiny path, then you will
be very well advised to pay attention to
material values and practical financial ideas,
for yours is a power number which stands for
organization, success and material freedom.
You came to be a power and a success, but in
order to do this you have to be prepared to
work hard, organize and exercise sound
judgement.

If you find yourself in a narrow
unrewarding type of life, then somewhere
you have missed out and should if possible go
back and find the right turning. You came to
head activities, to work for a goal or purpose,
and to use your energy and ambition
constructively for the good of the community
as a whole.

Certainly you can be successful, for you have poise, assurance and self-control, which would best be used in the commercial, financial or political realm. Prosperity and economic progress are keywords for your destiny path, and if you do not push too hard and have other than purely material values, you will be a great success.

A 9 Path of Destiny – Universal Love – Service
To be happy and successful with a number 9 destiny you have to cultivate a broadminded attitude to life as a whole. You have to forget petty little things which may and often do upset others, but which you should not allow to influence you, for your path will ask of you compassion, understanding and a broad service.

You should make your scope as wide as possible, associate yourself with some humanitarian scheme; national and international movements sometimes call number 9.

You will find that it is always you who is left to tie up the loose ends and to see a project through to completion, but this is your job, to cultivate a wide vision and an interest in what is going on in the world.

Success and happiness come to you in so far as you are able to forget your prejudices and really treat others as you would like to be treated yourself.

This is not a money vibration but moneywise you are divinely protected provided you live up to your ideals.

THE MASTER NUMBERS

Number 11 Destiny Number

If you have this number and do not wish to live up to its high potency, you can simply reduce it to a 2 and read there your destiny.

If, however, you wish to explore the heights and depths of number 11, you have to learn to trust your intuitions and guide your inventive and original mind into practical channels, that is if you wish to benefit from your ideas.

Certainly you will not have a dull life, but you will have to meet opposition in various guises throughout your life.

The mystical scene and its adherents are bound to cross your path at some time in your career, and you would be advised to allow your intuitions to guide you when this occurs. For you the unusual attracts, with all its implications.

You will be successful if you develop a philosophical attitude to life and are always guided by your own inner light.

You will come up against a dead end if you allow the power of this master number to drive you into being an eccentric and an impractical dreamer, or a critical, bossy worrier.

Number 22 Destiny Number

As with the other master number, 11, you can reduce a 22 to a 4, and read for yourself what is written there.

However, if you wish to live up to your full potential then you should be prepared to unite your ideals and your practical skills in some broad universal, idealistic scheme. This is a number which often occurs in relation to social welfare schemes and spiritual or healing foundations where the idealistic/humanitarian vision is to the fore.

You, in fact, were born to be the practical builder and idealist to bring down to earth your imaginative and constructive visions. New movements are your strong point.

However, you can only succeed if you see your ideas as a whole, allow others to work out the details and do not allow yourself to be sidetracked by others worried about the 'where' or the 'how'. You are the builder, so you must build somehow around, through or over your obstacles.

CHAPTER FOUR

THE MEANING OF YOUR BIRTHDAY VIBRATIONS

You are all interested in the interpretation of your birthday. From the numerological angle this has added significance as it is one of the most important cycles of life – the middle cycle. Therefore your birthday has considerable influence in choosing your career, and its vibration has to be considered also.

All birthdays are grouped into three classes called concords. They are the water, fire and air concords.

Water or Scientific Concords are those whose birthdays reduce to 1, 5 or 7. Since this is an element of mind, those who are born under these numbers require a good education, they make good writers, engineers or diagnosticians.

The water birthdays of any month are the 1st, 5th, 7th, 10th, 14th, 16th, 19th, 23rd, 25th and 28th. Number 1 people are go-ahead, intellectual, scientific and creative. Number 5 people are versatile, changeable and restless. Number 7 people are retiring, cautious and observant. All three are intuitive.

Fire or Business Concords. These are birthdays which reduce to 2, 4, 8, 11 or 22. People born under these numbers succeed best in the business humanitarian field.

However, musicians and conductors are sometimes born under these numbers owing to their gifts of timing and precision. This concord represents feeling and emotion. People born under these numbers feel deeply, but are unable to express their emotions, so are often misunderstood.

The business birthdays of any month are the 2nd, 4th, 8th, 11th, 13th, 17th, 20th, 22nd, 26th, 29th and 31st. They make good business executives, bankers, general merchants, secretaries, auditors and politicians, and innovators of new movements, especially 11 and 22.

Air or Artistic Concord. Those of you whose birthdays reduce to 3, 6, 9 are the artistic, literary and creative ones.

Your career lies before the public in some capacity. People born under these vibrations usually have no difficulty in expressing themselves in a creative way.

The element of air is spirit so these are regarded as the inspirational impersonal type.

The air birthdays of any month are the 3rd, 6th, 9th, 12th, 15th, 18th, 21st, 24th, 27th and 30th.

People born under this vibration make

good artists, writers, doctors, lawyers, advertisers, humanitarians and actors.

The meaning of a birthday is the same whatever the month or year of birth.

In interpretation it cannot stand alone, but must be considered with the destiny path, the ambition number and the expression number. Its influence helps you to find your true vocation.

Born on the 1st

You are a natural leader, strong-willed, independent, you like to go your own way and hate to be told that you are wrong.

It is difficult to appeal to your affections, but you like others to show you affection.

You are intellectually inclined and should have more than one iron in the fire. Your reasoning powers are excellent, and you are a good organizer.

Beware of jealousy and dominance.

You need to be the creative pioneer.

Born on the 2nd

You are the natural diplomat and work best with others rather than alone.

You love music, rhythm, dancing and have a natural sense of harmony, and appreciation of the fine and beautiful things in life.

The right environment makes or mars you, and you must be careful not to indulge in depression. Underestimation of your abilities could be a big handicap – assess yourself fairly, too.

Artistic or business lines are best.

Born on the 3rd

You are very gifted and must have individual self-expression in order to keep happy.

Social life and friends are the breath of life to you, so you are a social asset and sought after.

Gifted with a keen mind and lots of imagination, you should write, lecture, teach or find a place in journalism.

Your best outlet is in the intellectual, artistic, creative field.

Born on the 4th

You are a very firm, determined and sometimes stubborn person. You do not like to change your mind or your methods, but your gifts lie in the practical field and you are a hard worker, systematic, loyal and conscientious.

You tend to tell the truth even when it is unpalatable, and may make yourself enemies in this way.

Your emotional nature is well under control, others sometimes do not notice it, so give you less affection than you crave.

You always finish what you start, so any work requiring attention to detail, discipline and stamina would suit you, but basically the business world is best.

Born on the 5th

Versatile, quick in mind and body – that is you. You can turn your hand to many things but you hate to be confined. Routine is not for you.

You are one of life's enthusiasts and you enjoy every minute of it. Travel will come into your life owing to your innate restlessness.

Any work which keeps you on the go will please you, and owing to your enthusiasm you would make a good salesman or promoter.

It might be a good thing to settle young, but oh dear, heaven help your partner, because you hate to be restricted. With your enthusiastic, magnetic approach, you will have to learn to handle the opposite sex or else you will get your fingers burnt.

Any field which brings you before the public would suit you in some capacity where there was movement and action.

Born on the 6th

You are the home lover and need companionship, love and encouragement to give of your best. Under adverse conditions youngsters born under this number can get into considerable trouble and lose their confidence.

You have a pleasant speaking voice which could possibly be trained, and you are interested in music and the arts.

You would do well in any group or

community affairs, for you are an idealist and an improver of conditions in whatever capacity you find yourself.

Health, beauty, music or the stage are your best bets.

Born on the 7th

You are the introspective, quiet, analytical type. Your aim is perfection and the best of everything, for you are discriminating and not easy to know, although friendly once you know a person.

Your attraction is towards the scientific or the occult, for you are extremely psychic and sensitive and should follow your hunches.

Partnerships are your difficulty, as you are not an adaptable person nor truly domesticated.

Specialized pursuits are best for you.

Born on the 8th

If you were born on the 8th your real place is in the business world. You have innate good judgment, poise and the capacity to wield authority.

This is a good financial birthday, but if other factors in your numberscope are out of harmony you may have to struggle against adverse circumstances at some time in your life.

You like power, money and the 'big' situation, you are not interested in the mediocre, it follows you like to make a show.

You need some organization to be

successful, for it is within such a structure that your own powers and capacities are at their best.

Born on the 9th

You have both intellect and creative capacity so some broad field of activity is best for you. The 9 being a 'world' vibration, it is likely to bring considerable travel into your life, or occasion you to have to do with travel or communication in some form.

You are essentially impressionable, generous and protective, so you have to beware giving too much to the wrong people.

The wider your viewpoint the happier you are; you can reach for recognition in any artistic or professional field.

Born on the 10th

You were born to lead and to be independent so do not look for support from others, rather know that they will lean on you.

Nor should you try to work in harness with others, it will not work, you are the individualist and can handle several different lines at once provided you are at the head of the ventures.

Cultivate your artistic abilities as well.

Any individual enterprise is best for you, you have enough determination to get on in whatever field you choose.

Born on the 11th

This is a master birthday, and if it is yours

you have high ideals and aspirations.

Your difficulty is that you often allow your reason to overshadow your intuition. This will not do for you are extremely sensitive and psychic and should go on your hunches.

As this is a master number you come under a high vibration and will have to learn to keep your balance, even when your nerves are strung to breaking point. Emotional control and following the middle way are necessary for health and happiness. In spite of your above-average intelligence, allow your intuitions to function and find an unusual outlet for your great potential.

Born on the 12th

You have a warm, friendly personality, a practical mind and artistic or literary talent. Provided your surroundings are sufficiently interesting and your love life on an even keel, you can be a charming entertainer and a real whizz at promotion or salesmanship.

However, if love affairs and friendships are causing trouble you are all awry and discouraged, for these take pride of place in your life.

The entertainment or literary world suits you best.

Born on the 13th

You sometimes put your worst foot forward so that people misunderstand you and think you hard and dictatorial, for you find difficulty in expressing your feelings. A hard worker yourself and ambitious, you like to organize and manage others, having a flair for detail and scientific and mechanical leanings. Try and express your feelings more, use your imagination, and if possible cultivate a hobby such as wood carving or sculpture.

Born on the 14th
You are versatile and dual natured, having both a logical and imaginative mind. You can build or destroy, so powerful is the force of your birthday. You stand with one foot on earth and one in the starry heavens, so you can forge a true inspirational link between the two.

You love the new and original, change and variety; this could lead you to over-experiment in many fields, but really you need some stability and can then manage your career most successfully.

Born on the 15th
You are co-operative, giving and sympathetic, always willing to help and bear responsibility if called upon, but you must never stay in an environment where you feel dominated, for this would affect your health and well-being. You have an appreciation of all that is good and beautiful in life and crave a happy home and a kind, gentle mate who will allow you to be yourself. You would be best in some artistic or professional field.

Born on the 16th

This is a spiritual number, so links you with spiritual truths and philosophies rather than mundane affairs, although your inspirational and practical mind could lead you to seek success in a business career. However, your gifts lie along the development of your perhaps latent literary, artistic or musical gifts.

You are a perfectionist, so can get irritable, moody and depressed if you fail to reach your high standards. You need a home where you can be independent as well as loving.

Born on the 17th

Your variations in mood and attitude can be quite considerable. However, family and loved ones mean a great deal to you, and you are sensitive and emotional where your private life is concerned, if a trifle dominant in your business affairs.

Yours is considered a fine birthday from the point of view of finance. You would be wise to make your own decisions and to leave the details to lesser mortals. You should never want for lack of cash if you use your abilities rightly.

Born on the 18th

You are independent, efficient and a born leader. Intellectual matters are of interest to you and you find arguments congenial.

You have an emotional, sensitive side to your nature which gives you a love of music, but you tend to be critical and demanding.

It would be best if you used this analytical critical ability in your work as a critic or writer. You can expect an active life and much travel.

Born on the 19th

You are an extremist, subject to fluctuating moods running the gamut from 1 to 9. You live your life on the edge of a precipice, an emotional one, but you have tremendous resources and can weather all difficulties.

Use your original ideas and versatility and you will never want, but you should avoid being too set on your own way or you will have many knocks in your life. Choose your mate with care, for your birthday can bring you many misunderstandings in the married state.

Born on the 20th

You are above all an emotional type. You need friends, companionship and the comfort and backing given by others. You seek security, home and family and would do well in a family business, where your capacity for detail would be an asset.

You have musical or artistic talents and should try to cultivate them.

Try and avoid being overswayed by your emotions, for then you will get yourself a reputation for changeability. Success comes to you through cultivating your natural capacity for sympathy and patient handling of detail.

Born on the 21st

To be really happy you must have some means for personal self-expression through literature or the arts.

You are tactful and charming, but a definite individualist and independent. You may have an inclination to scatter your forces and waste your energies in too many directions at once.

You need beauty around you of colour and form, and make a good host or hostess.

As you are so up and down emotionally, love makes a big impact on your life for good or ill. In general you like to be on the receiving end of this rather than the giver.

The literary educational world is your best bet, and you can rest yourself by reading and relaxing, as well as enjoying entertainment and social life.

Born on the 22nd

It is your fortune or misfortune, according to the way you like to look at it, to be born on a master birthday, so you did not come here solely or even particularly for yourself.

Your aim was to leave the world the better for your passing through, so it follows that you should keep your mental balance and your feet on the ground, but interest yourself in anything which is for the public good –

humanitarian causes or welfare schemes are
within your capacity.

Your ideas cause you to look to wider
fields than the average, but you have to be
courageous and willing to keep your eyes on
your ideals, but yourself on this good earth.

If you feel you are not yet up to this, read
your birthday as under a 4 birthday.

Born on the 23rd

You are independent, self-sufficient, proud
and responsible.

You are a quick thinker when up against a
problem, your insight is remarkable and you
have the capacity to diagnose disease in the
body politic of an organization or else in the
physical body.

You get on better with the opposite sex
than with your own and with older rather
than younger people. You have the gift of
adaptability to changes in your
circumstances and environment.

Being versatile, you could venture into
business, the entertainment world or the
medical profession.

Born on the 24th

Your energy is quite stupendous, you must
always be on the move and active all your
life. You are prepared to take responsibility,
especially within the family or community,
for this is where your real interest lies.

You have the faults of your virtues of
energy and responsibility for you can be

worrying and jealous, determined that what you think is right should be done.

You can certainly work hard to achieve your aims, which possibly lie in the educational field.

Born on the 25th

You are the intuitive, inspirational type and conceal your thoughts and feelings, so are often misunderstood. You need to succeed for your own self-esteem, for you tend to set yourself standards of perfection and worry and grow moody when you fail. Never underestimate yourself.

These are influences which could steer you along creative lines and into salesmanship, but you have to concentrate and avoid being melancholy and erratic.

Town and bright lights are not really for you, you need the country and a simple life to be happy and successful.

Born on the 26th

You love home and children first, all the rest comes second in your life.

In spite of this you can succeed in the business field, for you are an excellent organizer and executive. You have great enthusiasm for starting things but do not find it so easy to finish them, so you need more continuity and persistence.

Pride of place and position are strong, so I don't advise marriage except to someone monied or likely to be so. Don't live in the

past and try and keep your emotions from
tearing you apart.

Born on the 27th

You have strength, determination and high
ideals, so you are a natural for leadership.
This you should remember in your life and
strive for the top or for working on your own,
the position of underling or of a 50/50
partnership will not suit you.

In friendship and marriage you have much
to give in terms of companionship and
affection. Your psychic sense is strong and
your birthday is likely to draw you to
metaphysics and philosophy.

Your main problem is that when things go
awry you can indulge your moods of
introversion and blind dislike; control this
and relationships go well. The literary or
artistic is best for you.

Born on the 28th

Your birthday indicates you have a strong
character and prefer the unconventional
within the confines of the conventional. You
are dominant, independent and ambitious
and should work in some individual capacity,
yet within some group of organization.

You are inclined to dream, then work
towards your ideals. Having attained them
you tend sometimes to lose interest.

Freedom is very important to you, but you
often find yourself hemmed in and are not
inclined to play this down, in fact you can

make quite a thing of it, keeping your troubles with you long after they can really be relinquished.

The unusual interests you.

Born on the 29th

In numerology this is considered a master birthday. It is a day which tends to bring you before the public, for you are intuitive and idealistic, with strong leadership qualities.

Unfortunately you are inclined to be moody and changeful, for you feel things strongly; with you the good is very good and the bad exceedingly bad.

You live on an emotional seesaw, so are not particularly easy to live with or understand. Interests outside your work can be soothing and help you to maintain your calm and poise. You need an outlet for your artistic, dramatic sense, perhaps through music or writing. You can be tremendously successful if other factors in your numberscope agree.

Born on the 30th

You were born with a great gift of imagination, so that this is the factor that you will use to find your self-expression, which is so important to your happiness. Drama or literature seem obvious outlets, but never try to force yourself into a routine job, for you will rue it.

Others should know that it is useless to argue with you, they will get nowhere, you have your own ideas and are not going to change them. At times you can be a bit erratic, but you make a good friend and are popular.

As you have strong ideals, some form of social work could appeal. Really any work which gives scope for your artistic talents is good for you too. Your danger is you can do many things well, but incline to impatience and the wasting of your energies.

Born on the 31st

You are a constructive type and can work hard to make yourself and family secure. Extremely loyal as a friend or worker, you can be stubborn and disinclined to alter either ways or opinions after the first part of life.

You need others and a firm family background in order to succeed, but will enjoy travel when the opportunity presents itself.

Remember not to aim too high, make your ambitions reasonable, then you will not suffer so many disappointments. Your birthday gives you a natural understanding of drugs and herbs and an interest in health and healing, and in this way you can help yourself at times.

Your success lies in making a good foundation to all you attempt.

CHAPTER FIVE

HOW TO LAY OUT AND ANALYSE YOUR NUMBERSCOPE

Books sometimes are frustrating teachers, for their writers often seem to forget the one little thing which it is essential to know in order to gain competency in any particular subject. You are left tearing your hair and the writer is quite unaware of your frustration.

In this book I aim to avert this situation, although it is difficult within a confined space, by explaining exactly how you should set up your numberscope.

If you will remember, the name totals gave us three factors.

1. The addition of the vowels gives the drive, ambition or inner desire.
2. The addition of the consonants gives the personality or the impression you make on others.
3. The addition of the vowels and consonants gives your expression number or what you do best, and your general mental approach.
4. The addition of the expression and the destiny gives the reality number, or your goal in this life, towards which you are working all your life.

Y is to be treated as a vowel only when there is no vowel in the name. Remember to check your arithmetic. It is no use unless correct in every detail.

Your destiny pattern is shown by the complete birthdate. That is the day, month and year of birth reduced to a single digit.

The name to be taken is always the one you were given at birth, even if this has been changed since for whatever reason.

The birthday is the one which applies at your meridian of birth.

Name changes bring additional vibrations but do not alter the birth pattern completely.

We now have a full example of name and destiny pattern.

```
1     5 +   6 3 9  5 +   6   5      = 6+5+11 = 22 =
A N N E  L O U I S E  J O N E S           4 = Ambition
  5 5  + 3       1 + 1   5   1     = 1+4+7 = 12 =
                                          3 = Impression
Addition of Ambition and Impression = 4+3 = 7 = Expression
```

Birthdate = Destiny Pattern, i.e. 2.4.1946 = 2+4+2 = 8 *Destiny*
Reality = Addition of 7 Expression and 8 Destiny = 15 = 6

What You Are Working Towards

The addition of these two gives you what you are working towards achieving in this life, it is always part of your character, but becomes increasingly so as life advances and has therefore greater relation to the second half of life.

The discovery of the 'Reality' is due to the research done by Dr Juno Jordan at the California Institute of Numerical Research.

Through twenty-five years of research Dr

Jordan proved the principles of names and numbers. His teachings have been my own unfailing source of knowledge, although I must admit that on one tenet I do not agree and that is in the use of the birth number as the birth force instead of the destiny number.

We can see that Anne Jones's deepest desire is for security and a practical approach to all the problems of her life (4 ambition, 8 destiny).

Although she has a pleasant, friendly, talkative personality (3 impression) giving the impression she has not a care in the world, in her inmost self she is a most practical, loyal and conscientious person (22/4 ambition). However her 3 impression may draw her to the more lighthearted and easy-going people and to those who will let her down or cause her pain especially in love, for the 3 in often frivolous and socially minded, but not very serious.

Although she can be the life and soul of the party, note her 3 impression, she is not a really sociable or adaptable person. In a close relationship she will be receptive, secretive, 'choosey' and introverted, the 7 expression.

She will not make many close friends, although she may have many acquaintances, but once she has made you a friend, you will find her loyal and self-sacrificing.

The Planes of Expression

We now have to deal with other factors

which give us more comprehensive insights into a person's temperament and aptitudes. These are referred to as the planes of expression.

Taking our previous example:

```
1    5 +   6 3 9  5 +  6   5    = 6+5+11 = 22 =
A N N E   L O U I S E   J O N E S              4 = Ambition
  5 5   + 3       1  + 1   5   1   = 1+4+7 = 12 =
                                          3 = Impression
4 Ambition + 3 Impression = 7 Expression
```

we total these, keeping in mind the meanings of the numbers.

In numberology, man's nature is divided into:
1. The physical numbers 4 and 5.
2. The emotional numbers 2, 3 6.
3. The mental numbers 1 and 8.
4. The intutional numbers 7 and 9.
   The name is set out like this:

A N N E   L O U I S E   J O N E S
1 5 55   3 6 3 9 1 5   1 6 5 5 1

Then we find 4 x 1s
            0 x 2s
            2 x 3s
            0 x 4s
            6 x 5s
            2 x 6s
            0 x 7s
            0 x 8s
            1 x 9s

We can now formulate another little table:

Physical   = 6 (only 5s)
Emotional = 4 (addition of 2s, 3s and 6s)
Mental   = 4 (addition of 1s and 8s)
Intutional = 1 (addition of 7s and 9s)

As mentioned earlier, the frequency with which numbers appear in a name, and their lack, both tell a tale and are very important in assessing temperament and aptitude.

Life will put us in the way of making up our lacks, yet we operate easily on the planes where we have many numbers, sometimes too easily. A high number on any plane gives the possibility of success and shows an outstanding individual talent along the lines of the number and its plane of expression.

One exception really is the 5, for this is such a restless number, and overbalance of 5s can vitiate success and make for Jack of all trades and master of none.

Interpretation of Anne's Numberscope

We see that this is exactly what we have here on Anne Louise's numberscope. She lacks the balance of 2s, 4s, 8s and 7s. Even if these are found in other parts of the chart, she will still be lacking to a certain extent.

The lack of 4s shows that she does not like detail, and is not too keen on hard work and method.

The lack of 2s and quite a few 1s shows she

is an individualist, has her own ideas and will stick to them, but does not find co-operation with others easy. This is again borne out by the expression number.

She has to learn organization and judgement as well as attention to practical values, she may either fear poverty and incline to miserliness or else be completely improvident.

Her destiny number shows that the business realm and commercial activity are her best bet vocationally, so to succeed she will have to develop her ability to deal with practical worldly things.

Repressed Emotions

Where in the planes of expression you find a 7 or the lack of it you can be pretty sure that your subject represses his emotions. This is bad for nerves, health and ordinary general human intercourse. There is a shrinking from expressing the motions for fear of finding the affections repulsed or treated lightly.

A barrier is built up between the self and other human beings, the person is lonely and may seek outlets in other ways such as drink, drugs, promiscuity or ill health.

The advice to be given is, 'Don't take yourself too seriously. Yes, you may be hurt, but you'll be in the same boat as every other human being. Don't let pride and coldness of heart turn you into an "icebox".'

Now we will just analyse the birthdate and the influence of the birthday.

8 – an Extrovert Number

We have already said that the 8 was a 'mind' number and one related to the conquest of the material place, an extrovert number. This will not be an easy road for Anne Jones, for she is introvert in 'expression' and so will be unlikely to like the noise, dash and rush of the day by day commercial world.

However, Anne could go into an organization which had to do with the arts, creative work of any kind such as music, and she will not mind taking responsibility, for she has two 6s on her physical plane.

Anne can speak well, the 6 has to do with the voice, so she would quite like a job which gave her enough scope for variety, many people coming in and out; she has six 5s on the planes, little routine and some time to herself.

She would cope with others pleasantly, would like nice surroundings and a fairly free hand, she would make an excellent P.R.O. for she is able to keep her mouth shut (7 on the expression), and be diplomatic and tactful (2 on birthday).

Anne can also carry responsibility and provided she got the encouragement and thanks that her nature requires to do her best (6 on the physical plane), she would be happy, especially if her work was well

enough paid to allow her to bank some of her
money, although with that number of 5s on
the planes of expression she will very likely
learn economy the hard way, for the 5s and
the 3s are the spendthrifts of the chart.

Her difficulties in life will come from the
divergence between the 7 of her expression
and the 8 of her destiny.

The 8 will tend to push her out into
circulation and the 7 will hold her back,
making her reticent and secretive.

4 – Ambition Number

However, she has a 4 ambition number in
tune with her other business numbers, the 2
of her birthday and the 8 of her destiny.

At the same time, her physical
attractiveness and her charm of manner,
indicated by her physical plane 6 will enable
her to function in an outgoing manner and
attract to herself in love and friendship those
who can make her happy if she will curb the
moodiness of her 7 expression and use it
positively to enable her to see beneath the
surface of the people and situations she will
have to meet in life.

As a last note on the analysis of the name
and birthdate, it is wise to remember that
any number can be used positively or
negatively. The positive expression of a
number harmonizes with a situation, the
negative expression is always separative,
limited and selfish.

When laying out a chart, work everything

out on one sheet of paper, including future indications which we shall be going into in the next chapter, for then you will be able to assess the present reaction of the person from the natal data and the existing indications.

CHAPTER SIX

AND WHAT ABOUT YOUR FUTURE?

When you have drawn up the birth chart and you want a fairly quick assessment of whether the life will be easy or difficult, draw up a sort of box arrangement rather like the game of noughts and crosses which, no doubt, some of you used to play as children. The following diagram shows which number goes where.

3	6	9
2	5	8
1	4	7

Along the top line are arranged the numbers 3, 6, 9 from left to right.

Along the second horizontal line are arranged the numbers 2, 5, 8 from left to right.

Along the third horizontal line are arranged the numbers 1, 4, 7 from left to right.

You will notice that along the *horizontal columns* the numbers are 3 degrees apart in mathematical value. This implies many problems and a hard road to gain success.

Along the *vertical columns* the numbers are 1 and 2 degrees apart. There is little stretch between them. This shows that life will not be too hard. Not so much effort will have to be put in to make a success of life. You'll get along.

Along the *diagonal column* of 1, 5, 9 the stretch is 4 points or degrees. There will be ease of accomplishment, perhaps too much ease, too little struggle to bring out strength of character. Downfall through taking life too easy, depending too much on others.

In this quick look only the numbers of the birthdate are used. For example we have a birthdate of 6 February 1950. So we put out 6.2.1950.

The 6 goes in the second column on the first line. The 2 on the first column of the second line.

Taking the numbers now of the year, we put 1 on the bottom line left-hand corner. The 9 in the right-hand top corner and the 5 in the central diagonal.

	6	9
2	5	
1		

As you can see at a glance, this person will have a relatively easy life. Things come to him; he does not have to make much effort. His danger is of taking it too easily; of wasting both his time and his money on easy living – notice that the birthdate itself adds up to the 5, the spendthrift and the lover of change and variety.

Your Future Indications

Now for the future and your means of looking at your future indications.

There are important divisions of life known technically as 'pinnacles'. These are computed by:

1. First subtracting the destiny number from 36.
This gives the period of the first pinnacle.
The *first pinnacle number* is found by the addition of the day and month and has a duration of nine years.
2. Find *the second pinnacle* by adding together the day and year of birth. It too has a duration of nine years.
3. Now add together the addition of the previous two and this gives *the third pinnacle*; also of nine years duration.
4. To find the *fourth and final pinnacle*, add the month and year of birth. This together with the first pinnacle is the longest and lasts from the end of the third pinnacle to the end of life.

The *pinnacles* show the kind of attitude and the type of experience to be encountered over the period of time they last.

Naturally in every case the additions must be reduced to a single digit. A further refinement is given by the potential shown by the day, month and year of birth. These are called *cycles*, and they add a little more knowledge since they show the environment and the situation, or background to the pinnacles.

The *first cycle* is the month number and lasts as long as the first pinnacle.

The *second cycle* is the date number and lasts through the second and third pinnacles and the first nine years of the fourth pinnacle. This is called the *cycle of productivity* and is considered the most important as it is usually the most active period of a person's life.

Besides the cycles, pinnacles and personal year number, which is found by adding the addition of the day and month of birth to the universal year number (addition of digits of the year), we also have the 'weak links' in a person's character, pitfalls which can ruin the life or take away from success and happiness.

These are called *challenges*, and are found by subtraction from the cycle numbers. These too run concurrently with the pinnacles.

From these indications and others which it is not possible to discuss in a book of this size, a pretty fair idea of the life pattern and trends ahead can be found.

As these instructions have been pretty condensed I will give an example of the way in which the future can be laid out according to these guidelines.

To interpret these you can use also the meanings given to the various numbers in earlier chapters, although I do give a summary.

Numbers always have the same meanings,

only their position on the chart or the progressed chart change. In order to be a good analyst you have to understand their meanings and apply these with understanding and intuition to the whole chart including the birth chart.

No indication stands on its own, one person will not react in the same way to the stresses set up by similar vibrations. How they react will depend upon the strength or weakness of the number (characteristic) in their birth chart, so I advise making the whole work out on one sheet so that you could easily check up this strength or weakness.

Example of Progress Chart
Now we will take an example of a progress chart to see the future trends ahead.

the birthdate is $\underset{3+4+7}{\underline{21.4.1942}} = 14 = 5$ destiny.

Find the Pinnacles
1. Subtract destiny number from 36 to find time of first pinnacle. $36 - 5 = 31$.
So first pinnacle = up till age 31.
2. Find *first pinnacle* by adding together the day and month of birth. $3 + 4 = 7 =$ first pinnacle.
3. Add the day and year, $3 + 7 = 10 = 1$. This is the *second pinnacle*.
4. *Add the addition of the previous two in order to find the third pinnacle.*

5. Add the month and year, 4 + 7 = 11 to find the *fourth pinnacle*.

Find the Cycles

1. The *first cycle*, which goes the length of the first pinnacle, is the month number.
2. The *second cycle*, which is the date number, runs through the second and third pinnacles and for nine years of the fourth pinnacle. The year number is the cycle for the rest of the fourth pinnacle.

Find the Challenges (the weaknesses which will be highlighted at particular times in the life)

1. Subtract the day and month of birth for the *first challenge*. This runs concurrently with first pinnacle and cycle. 3 – 4 = 1 so 1 is the *first challenge*.
2. Subtract the day and year numbers (always the higher from the lower of course) and so we take 3 – 7 = 4 so 4 is the number of the *second pinnacle challenge*.
3. Subtract the number of the first challenge from that of the second or vice versa, whichever is the higher, and you have the *challenge* for the *third pinnacle*.
4. Subtract the number of the year from that of the month for the *fourth challenge* to last till the end of life.

So diagrammatically this can be expressed as follows.

$$\text{Birthdate} = \frac{21.4.1942}{3 \quad 4 \quad 7} = 14 = 5 \text{ destiny.}$$

	Cycle	Pinnacle	Challenge
From birth to age 31 =	4	7	1
From age 32 to age 41 =	3	1	4
From age 42 to age 51 =	3	8	3
From age 52 to end of life =	3 for 9 years then 7 for rest of life.	11	3

So the first and last pinnacles are the longest, the others being of nine years' duration, and indicate the environment and experiences which will form part of the life.

Short Explanation of the Meaning of the Pinnacles

1. Gives opportunity to be independent, an individual and at the head of things. Active period – person must stand on own feet. Sudden changes likely.

2. Work is to be found with others. Do not stand alone, co-operation and diplomacy are keywords here.

3. Cheerful time for travel, developing literary, creative or social abilities. Friendships mean much, and so does luxury. Don't be too lavish with love or money.

4. A practical period when it will be difficult to do more than stay on the job and attend to the duties of working or building for the future.

5. Free and changeful time, travel, contacts

and uncertainty, but a lively, interesting period of experience.

6. Usually a time when the individual has the opportunity to marry, build a home, have children. Relatives and responsibility are the keynotes.

7. An 'inturned' period of spiritual and mental growth. Soul development. Can be a lonely time and hard on the health. Good for specialization.

8. A good financial period if effort and discrimination are used. Good position and responsibility within an organization usually.

9. A period of opportunity to learn and understand a great deal about life. Disappointing on the personal level in connection with love, money or friendship. A hard lesson to be learnt to live for others unselfishly.

11. A time of successful forwarding of the ideals. Can apply to self or children who have creative successes.

22. A time when it will be possible to further schemes of vision and expansion, perhaps on an international scale.

The meaning of the cycles and the challenges is similar. In the case of the challenge it indicates that the person who, for instance, has a 3 challenge must bring out their creative and joyful side, they must express themselves creatively. Failure to do so will militate against happiness.

Likewise with the meaning of the cycles. A

4 cycle on a first pinnacle will indicate some hard work, study, getting down to it at school and university.

Every year a person's number vibration changes, and as mentioned earlier this is found by adding the day and month of your birth to the universal year number.

The year of 1971 was a 9 year for $1 + 9 + 7 + 1 = 9$. To find your own year which, taken in conjunction with your natal indications and the indications of the pinnacles, cycle and challenge, will show you what to expect of the year: you simply add your day and month of birth to 9. A person born on 5 May will add $5 + 5 = 1$, so in 1971 she was beginning a new cycle of living necessitating organizing well and making important decisions which will affect her future for the next nine years.

We can also look at any particular month and see what it promises for us. To find your personal month, add the number of your personal year to the calendar month.

CHAPTER SEVEN

LOVE, MONEY AND SUCCESS

The magic of Numbers can provide you with valuable information about your attitudes to love, money and success. The procedure is simple.

Concentrate on the word you have chosen (LOVE, MONEY or SUCCESS). Then spontaneously select in your mind any three numbers up to nine (you can include eleven and twenty-two if you like). Add them up and reduce to a single number (unless they come to eleven or twenty-two). Now check your number for its interpretation in the list of number totals given below.

Remember that you must be relaxed before you undertake this procedure and that your choice of three numbers must be spontaneous.

LOVE

Number One

This implies that you are sincere in feeling and that you are looking for the *ONE* person, the right one. Love must be romantic and far removed from the everyday world. Caution: you could be a bit selfish, which would militate against your happiness.

Number Two

You look for security first of all, this is because you want a home of your own, a family and children whom you can love and protect. You hate to do the chasing, want your love to come to you, but remember it does not do to be too diffident; you could miss out.

Number Three

Lighthearted is your attitude to love, you do not want to settle down, you want to enjoy yourself and sample what is offering. This may be a temporary feeling, nevertheless it is true for the moment. Do enjoy yourself.

Number Four

Your attitude to love is steady and loyal, you consider love as an extension of your attitude to friendship in general, that of stability and steadfastness. You will not have many love affairs in your life as you are the persistent type. You need a sincere and thrifty mate.

Number Five

You are someone who needs a family so you would not consider marrying someone who did not care for children. You also like romance and travel, which may mean that you are attracted to a mate from afar. Through your love affairs and in your marriage you want to learn a lot and so need someone who loves family, travel, education and physical fulfilment.

Number Six

You are the domestic type. First and foremost you want a home and a kind understanding mate. The practical aspects of marriage will always be important to you and you'll make sure that this is all arranged before you make the marriage arrangements. Your attitude is mature, loving and reasonable, so you should lead a happy life.

Number Seven

You are selective and discriminating in love and friendship, something of a loner as you look for perfection and the tiniest little thing can put you off. You are not convinced of the benefits of marriage or close relationship and your attitude is perhaps a little too critical and inhibited.

Number Eight

Your attitude to love includes the need for money. You are not one to say 'let's starve in a garret'. Love is very important to you, but for you love and money must go together. Do not stress the riches side too much or you might find yourself married to someone whose career comes first.

Number Nine

You have a giving nature and feel that love should expand your horizons and allow you to put some of your ideals into practice. You need someone with as wide and loving a heart as your own.

Number Eleven

You are attracted to the unconventional type of mate. You feel that the right person will come along, that this is part of your Destiny pattern. Do not be too passive about this, you need to mix like anyone else and cannot sit and wait for your lover to come to you out of the blue.

Number Twenty-two

You are the idealistic type and will not find it too easy to find the right mate as your early attitudes to sex may have become rather fixed and rigid, so making adjustment to partnership difficult. Loosening up on inhibitions will help you to find happiness.

MONEY

Number One

If this is your total, then money in itself is not of great interest to you, but you like to obtain it in original ways. It indicates that you gain most through your own creative efforts and by your contacts with people who know how to make money. All in all you put *LOVE* before *MONEY*.

Number Two

If this is your total, then to you money means *SECURITY*, especially in connection with the home, your family and children. If you do not think of it as an end in itself. When you use your diplomatic powers you gain financially, when you assert yourself and force issues you lose out.

Number Three
If this is your total, you think of money as luck, you tend to be a bit of a gambler and rather extravagant. In fact you find it hard to take money seriously. However, you could be lacking in consideration moneywise where others are concerned and, for instance, forget to pay your bills, as to you money matters are taken so lightheartedly. You are likely to be lucky, but remember those who are not.

Number Four
If this is your total, you take money seriously and are prepared to work to obtain it. However, you have a tendency to be insecure where your finances are concerned and to be rather pessimistic about your chances of obtaining enough money. You have to work for what you get, but don't let that make you too tightfisted.

Number Five
If this is your total, you like to use your money to finance your trips and you hope that these will involve you in romantic encounters. To find security you need to find some endeavour along the lines of communication such as writing, selling, being an agent or something in publishing. These are suggestions which might appeal to you and bring you security without tying you

down too much. Money and romance are likely to be yours.

Number Six

If you do not possess sufficient money you tend to worry, so to you money is necessary as an antidote to your own feelings of insecurity. You feel you need it for any worthwhile venture such as marriage, travel or any other enterprise. But you like to feel you'll always have enough money to help out those you love.

Number Seven

If this is your total, money and its handling is something of a mystery to you. You are not very practical or capable when it comes to coping with more than a few pounds. You may gain money from unexpected sources and out of the blue. You need to try and be more practical in your budgeting.

Number Eight

You are at ease in handling money and in managing your budget, as this comes naturally to you. You have big ideas and tend to judge people by their appearance of affluence or the opposite. You can be deceived this way as things are not always what they seem. Your desire to acquire money will ensure that you have plenty.

Number Nine

You hate to be short of cash. In some way

money, and a sufficiency of it, means that
you feel sure of yourself and confident. You
need it to fulfil your purposes and to express
yourself as you would want. You always aim
high and on the whole you'll succeed.

Number Eleven

If this is your total you like to obtain your
money in unusual ways and you are
singularly influenced by what others think of
you. In fact your need for money stems from
what you want others to think of you. How
they see you is most important to your own
sense of security. You'll gain most through
progressive techniques and perhaps through
the occult or alternative medicine.

Number Twenty-two

If this is your total, you like a broad view
where money is concerned and you see it as a
means for achieving success in big projects,
probably along commercial lines, for this is a
good field for you.

You need to be practical, then to stretch
your practicality a bit in order to achieve
your dreams of success.

SUCCESS

Number One

If your total is *ONE* you are not the type of
person to take the broad highway in life. To
seek success you will take up something new,
independent, progressive – and succeed.

Number Two
If this is your total, you are not exactly a go-getter. You like your leisure and pleasure too much. However, success could come to you through cultural fields, such as music, art, literature.

Number Three
You are naturally attracted to success, but having a vivid imagination you can explore many fields to achieve your ends and this implies you may scatter your talents, energies and forces too much. It is wise for you to limit your scope, to finish one project before you start another.

Number Four
If this is your total, you are one of the most practical of persons: where success is concerned you are prepared to work for it. Your attitude is realistic, but you can take success so seriously that you have little time for enjoyment.

Number Five
You are a creative type and look for your success along the lines of travel and excitement. The communication of ideas is important to your success. If your luck holds you could make yourself a household name as a writer, journalist or television commentator.

Number Six

If this is your total, then you do not desire any spectacular success. Your happiness is based upon success in the home, family, and in love. You are willing to let the rest go by if you can obtain these blessings. You are likely to do so.

Number Seven

You look for success through the realization of a dream partner who will share your ideals, hopes, joys and sorrows and with whom, of course, you will achieve success. Yours is the perfect dream of complete perfection. A difficult ideal to realize, but if you do you'll certainly be a lucky person.

Number Eight

If this is your total, to you success is *MONEY* with a capital 'M'. Your heart's desire lies with material things, clothes, cars, homes, good food and drink and the wherewithal to buy all these. You need to know how to share some of your 'goodies' with others and then you'll be happier and more fulfilled. You are a go-getter and likely to succeed.

Number Nine

If this is your total, you aim for international fame. You aim high and can best achieve success through the entertainment world, the creative arts or through your dedication to humanitarian ideals. You can make it.

Number Eleven

You dislike the beaten track and aim to achieve success in fields other than the usual ones. Actually, you are not likely to be too successful in any settled, well tried field. You could succeed in television, computers, ESP work or in any of the occult or New Age techniques.

Number Twenty-two

If this is your total, then you consider that your success lies in your own personal approach, persuasive tactics and actual magnetism. So you could well succeed in any field of selling, particularly along broad lines, as you can have the Midas touch.

If you are prepared to start all over again if you find you are barking up the wrong tree, you are sure to be successful in the long run.

CHAPTER EIGHT

LOVE WITHOUT TEARS

You have probably noticed that there is nothing in the world so important as relationships. We sink or swim according to the quality of our relationships, and relationships depend upon our ability to communicate.

Numerology gives a great deal of assistance in assessing whether we would be happier together or apart, whether the relationship can be ephemeral or permanent, but in order to find this out it is necessary to do out the full charts for both people and also to look at their present and future trends as discussed in the last chapter.

Broadly speaking there are three rules which show with what ease we will get along with other people.

		Water	Air	Fire
1.	Similars	1.5.7	3.6.9	2.4.11.22
2.	Complements	Two numbers, both odd or both even.		
3.	Opposites	Two numbers, one odd and one even and of different concords.		

The concords are water, air and fire, as shown above.

Similars: This brings harmony in close relationship. This is shown when the ambition number and the destiny are the same.

Complements: If two numbers are both odd or both even, then the two people will complement one another. Each will contribute what the other lacks.

Though the number vibrations are different, this is a harmonious set-up for each will learn and develop through the differences.

Opposites: If either the ambition number or the destiny number are opposite numbers, there will be great difficulty in understanding one another's ideals or sympathizing with one another's interests. There will be strong attraction, though each seeing in the other something entirely different and unknown. There will be strong personality clashes.

If you really understand the meaning of each of the numbers, then it will be easy for you to see when you first meet someone in what direction you will really 'hit it off'. Simply add the digit of your expression number to theirs and see what the resulting number is.

For instance, your expression number is 1 and his is 9. You then get a resulting 1. You can work, study, organize, begin new projects together.

Or yours is a 1 and his is 1, = 2; you'll

probably fall in love if the circumstances are conducive, marry, establish a home and family.

The same principle can be applied to the addition of two birthdates, day, month and year of birth. Yours adds up to a 6, his to a 9, = 6. Here you have mutual understanding; remember both belong to the same air concord and so are similars.

There can be mutual understanding which can make a lasting friendship, partnership, marriage or collaboration. Both will learn a great deal from the other, both will develop, improve and mature.

But if you are seriously interested, or shall we say *when* you are seriously interested, you must compare the two charts and study the pinnacles and cycles of life as well. On the whole if you are seriously interested it might be wise to get an expert numerologist to assess the pros and cons for you.

Another factor which will help you assess whether you and another person will get on well together is whether either is basically a positive, outgoing type or an intuitional, more creative person.

Positive and Negative

To help you assess this, numbers are divided into positive and negative. It is easy to remember that even numbers give positive, objective and basically extroverted characteristics. The odd numbers give negative, subjective, intuitional, feminine and introverted characteristics.

So when the even numbers predominate in a name and birthdate, it denotes a more negative, subjective, imaginative type. Expressed in a nutshell, the formers are 'doers', the latter 'thinkers'.

This, as you will realize, is too facile, for there are always various shades of white from grey to black and no one is entirely introverted or extroverted, but in general you will find there is some penchant towards one or the other.

For a predominantly introverted girl to get hooked up with a predominantly extroverted male *could* produce problems of communication, and so jeopardize the relationship unless both care enough to work at it.

Many people are interested in whether they will marry young, older or not at all. Others are interested in whether they will remarry, and these are two separate questions really.

6-Marriage Number

The number of marriage is 6, and when this number is predominant in the chart, that is either as the expression number or the destiny number, it is hard to see how these people are going to escape early marriage unless there are many introverted numbers to make the time at which they marry later than you would normally expect.

The years which are important for marriage are those personal years which add up to 3, 5, 6. The latter is a year which is more promising for a settled, secure future. The 5 brings a more jazzy vibration, tremendous physical attraction and sometimes rather a love/hate scene.

If a girl has a 6 expression, a 6 on her pinnacle and comes to a 6 personal year, she is more than likely to marry.

To consider remarriage, take the expression number into consideration. If this is an introvert number and the pinnacle number is also, then there is less likelihood of remarriage. A change of pinnacle will alter the picture perhaps.

Sometimes people marry late in life due to responsibilities or lack of money and security. To see whether they will, you have to look and see whether the pinnacle number is a 6 or a 2, and if so you can say fairly confidently that they will not be alone in their later years.

This is particularly so if the reality number, the addition of the destiny number and the expression, is a 6 or a 2.

In fact, with a 6 on the reality, a true and lasting love may not come until later in life, when at last the right person comes along.

The thing is that numerology can help you to understand other people. Although much has had to be condensed into a small space, and so it has naturally been impossible to go into the subject in great depth, even with the pointers given here I hope that perhaps some understanding will have been given as to the basic differences in our characters and in our destinies and ways of life. Anything that contributes to better understanding and so better relationships in depth and quality is worth looking into.

'Should I Change My Name?'

Lastly, a question often asked is, 'Should I change my name?' The answer is yes, if it will help you to succeed in a particular field. As you now know the meanings of the different number vibrations, you will know that certain numbers are good for business, certain numbers good for creative matters. Who has not heard of the singer who wilted away in the wilderness for seventeen years before changing his name and gaining instant success?

If you want to succeed in a creative/literary field, your name change should be to a 3.6.9. If it is business success you are after, you should go for an 8.

However, it is advisable to take the destiny and birthday into consideration so it might be wise to consult a professional if you feel you want or need a change of name. Remember, though, that this does not wash out the original name. This vibration always stands. The new name adds something of the quality which you need.

Finally, I hope you enjoy your study of numbers and find it great fun.

INDEX